DESIGN IT!

FOOD DESIGN

Alix Wood

Gareth Stevens
PUBLISHING

Please visit our website, **www.garethstevens.com**.
For a free color catalog of all our high-quality books,
call toll free 1-800-542-2595 or fax 1-877-542-2596

Cataloging-in-Publication Data
Names: Wood, Alix.
Title: Food design / Alix Wood.
Description: New York : Gareth Stevens Publishing, 2018. | Series: Design it! | Includes index.
Identifiers: ISBN 9781538208007 (pbk.) | ISBN 9781538207949 (library bound) |
   ISBN 9781538207826 (6 pack)
Subjects: LCSH: Food craft--Juvenile literature. | Food presentation--Juvenile literature.
Classification: LCC TT160.W66 2018 | DDC 745.5--dc23

First Edition

Published in 2018 by
Gareth Stevens Publishing
111 East 14th Street, Suite 349
New York, NY 10003

Produced for Gareth Stevens by Alix Wood Books
Designed by Alix Wood
Editor: Eloise Macgregor
Editor for Gareth Stevens: Kerri O'Donnell
Food stylists: Rebecca Wood; Ben Wood

Photo credits: Cover, 1, 7, 9, 18, 19, 20, 21, 22, 23, 24, 25, 26, 27, 28, 29, 30 © Ben Wood; Cover
(plate image)Max Maier ;4, 5, 6 © Adobe Stock Images; 10, 11, 14, 15, 16, 17, 32 © Rebecca Wood;
all other pictures © Alix Wood

Printed in the United States of America
CPSIA compliance information: Batch #CS17GS: For further information contact Gareth Stevens, New York, New York at 1-800-542-2595.

CONTENTS

DESIGN WITH FOOD

When top **chefs** create food for their customers, the food obviously needs to taste good — but it has to look great, too! Food that looks good makes you want to eat it. Chefs give the **presentation** of their food a lot of thought.

There are all kinds of ways to make food look interesting. You can decorate your food, arrange it in a special way, or make it into a sculpture. You can even carve patterns in it!

Food designers might work in a restaurant, or create food for film or TV productions. Some design amazing cakes for weddings or special occasions. Other food designers work for food magazines or book publishers.

Design Tips

Watermelon carving is a tradition in Thailand, China, and Japan. People have been doing it for hundreds of years. They can carve amazing patterns.

Making food look good in a photograph is not as easy as it seems. Trying to get a plate of spaghetti to behave itself is definitely an art! Food designers need to understand what will look good on camera. If food designers are working on a film or TV set, they also need to know what to do when things start melting under the hot **studio** lights.

Presentation is important! Which of these cupcakes would you want to give as a gift?

BLINDFOLD TASTE TEST

Do you think how food looks affects how it tastes? Try this test! Get some jellybeans of different flavors. Put on a blindfold. Have someone pass you a jellybean. Taste it and try to guess what flavor it is. It's not as easy as you think when you can't see the color of the candy!

LOOKS MATTER

Head chefs will check food prepared in their kitchen before it goes to customers. Any food that does not look good will be rejected. It has to be cooked perfectly and it has to look amazing.

FOOD SAFETY

It is really important to practice good **hygiene** around food. **Bacteria** in food such as raw meat can make you very ill. You can't see bacteria. Always wash your hands well after touching raw food and keep all your equipment and surfaces really clean.

Design Tips

Food stylists use strange tricks to make food look perfect under the hot studio lights. Ice cream melts really quickly, so stylists might make fake ice cream from fat and powdered sugar. Yuck! You wouldn't want to eat that!

Food stylists are very picky when they choose the food they photograph. They may spend hours choosing the perfect burger bun. Even then, it may not be good enough! Stylists sometimes use tweezers and glue to stick on extra sesame seeds so the bun looks just right!

MARZIPAN FRUIT

Try styling some food yourself! Marzipan "fruits" are fun to make. Marzipan is a treat made from almonds, sugar, and eggs.

YOU WILL NEED:
- marzipan (white marzipan works best)
- food coloring
- a toothpick

1

Make a small ball out of marzipan. Make a dent in the ball and drip in a few drops of green food color. Squish the marzipan around until the color looks even. Mix some red and blue color to make brown for the marzipan stalk.

2

To make your marzipan strawberry look realistic, poke tiny holes all over its surface using a toothpick. Use brown food coloring to add details to your marzipan banana!

GOOD PRESENTATION

Even when food looks fantastic, a messy plate can make a meal unpleasant! It's important to present your food well. Look through photographs in a good cookbook and you'll see lots of different ways to present food. Designers often use **props** in their photos. They usually choose props that match the country the food is from.

TABLE SETTING

In a fancy restaurant, it's not just the chefs that care about the details. Waiters will decorate the tables with flowers, tablecloths, and nice **cutlery** and **crockery**.

What country do you think this food might be from?

8

PLATE DECORATING

Even simple food can look amazing if it is presented on a decorated plate. Try it yourself.

1 To make the berry sauce, put a big handful of berries, a tablespoon of sugar, and a cup of water into a small pan. Bring the water to boil, then simmer until the fruit is soft.

YOU WILL NEED:
- a squeezy bottle or **pastry bag**
- berry sauce
- an adult to help you

2

Mix the ingredients in a blender. Add more water if it looks too sticky. Then strain through a sieve using the back of a ladle or spoon.

3 Spoon the berry sauce into the squeezy bottle or pastry bag. Now decorate your plate with patterns and dots.

Make these cupcakes on pages 22–23

LADYBUG BLT

Making food look fun can make it more of a pleasure to eat. Have you got a younger sibling who doesn't want to eat their vegetables? How about trying to tempt them with this cute ladybug BLT!

YOU WILL NEED:
- bacon
- tomato and lettuce
- black olives
- bread
- mayonnaise
- a frying pan
- a knife and chopping board

1

With an adult's help, fry your bacon so it is just how you like it. Pans can get hot and be dangerous.

2

Lightly toast a piece of bread. Place your slices of cooked bacon on top.

3

Wash some lettuce and then pat it dry using a paper towel. Place the lettuce on the bacon.

4 Ask an adult to help you. Slice the tomato, and cut the olives in half. Keep one olive whole to use as the ladybug's head.

5 Cut a tomato slice in half to form the ladybug's wings. For the spots, place some sliced olives on the wings. Place one olive at the front for the head.

Make **antennae** from small strips of lettuce stalk. Make the eyes using two dots of mayonnaise and tiny pieces of black olive.

Food designers often present their food on a plain, white plate. Why do you think that is?

CAKE DECORATING

There are so many ways that you can decorate a cake. Check out these easy chocolate cake designs! See if you can think up your own, too.

YOU WILL NEED:
- an iced chocolate cake
- chocolate finger cookies
- colorful chocolate candies
- a knife and plate

Measure your chocolate cookies against the side of the cake. If they are too tall, cut a little off one end of each cookie.

2

Start to arrange the chocolate cookies around the edge of the cake. You can use a little of the icing to help stick them in place.

3

Keep adding the cookies until you are almost all around the cake. Then, cut a slice out of the cake to create a gap.

4

Sort your candy into colors. Decorate the top of your cake, and pile the rest of the candy in the gap.

Design Tips

Another great way to design a cake is to top it with decorations or slices of small Swiss rolls. These two chocolate cakes look and taste really good, too!

MARSHMALLOW PENGUINS

These marshmallow penguins are so cute. Maybe you could put them on an iced, snow-themed cake? Or you could present them on a board sprinkled with powdered sugar!

YOU WILL NEED:
- marshmallows
- baking chocolate
- chocolate candies
- a mixing bowl
- a spoon
- a spatula
- black and white tubes of icing

1

Break up the chocolate into small pieces and place them in a microwave-safe bowl.

2

Ask an adult to help you. Put the bowl in a microwave for 1 minute, or until the chocolate melts. Check and stir it often. You and an adult can also melt the chocolate in a bowl in a pan of boiling water.

3

When the chocolate has melted, stir it until it is smooth. Then leave the mixture to cool for a few minutes. You want the chocolate to be cool, but still a little runny.

4

Now start to make the penguin shape on the marshmallows. Dip a spatula in the chocolate mixture. Carefully paint the chocolate onto the marshmallow, leaving a white area for the penguin's face.

5

Carefully cut some orange chocolate candies in half to use as beaks. Stick them on using a little melted chocolate.

Make the eyes using the tubes of black and white icing.

OWL PANCAKES

Try making these fun pancake owls for breakfast!
They are cute, healthy, and pretty easy to make.
Ask an adult to help you cook,
as the skillet needs to be hot
to cook the pancakes.

For the pancakes
YOU WILL NEED:
- 1 cup sifted flour
- 2 tablespoons of sugar
- 1 cup milk
- 2 teaspoons baking powder
- half a teaspoon of salt
- 1 large egg
- vegetable oil
- a whisk, a bowl
- a skillet and a spatula

1

Whisk together the milk, butter or oil, and the egg.

2

Add the flour, baking powder, and sugar. Whisk until just mixed.

3

Heat the skillet. Put some oil in the pan. Drop in a tablespoon of pancake mix. Cook for 1–2 minutes on each side.

For the toppings
YOU WILL NEED:
- a banana
- strawberries
- blueberries
- maple syrup
- a knife and chopping board

1

You may need an adult to help cut the fruit. Cut the banana into slices. Remove the stalks from the strawberries and cut them lengthwise into slices. These will become your owls' beaks and wings.

2

Now add your eyes, beak, and wings. **Drizzle** on some maple syrup and enjoy!

Design Tips

To make your blueberries sit nicely on the banana slices, you could slice the blueberries in half.

SPOOKY FOOD

Sometimes you want your food to look really horrible — horribly scary! It's fun to design some spooky food to creep out your friends on Halloween. Try these stuffed pepper pumpkins!

1

With an adult's help, cut the tops off a couple of orange bell peppers. Keep the tops on one side. Scrape the seeds out of the middle of the pepper and throw them away.

2

Now carve a face on the pepper, just like a Halloween pumpkin! You will need an adult to help you do this. Draw your face onto the pepper by pressing into the skin with a toothpick, then ask an adult to cut out your design using a knife.

Design Tips

Keep your pumpkin face design simple. Peppers are small, and once they are cooked, any tiny details may be hard to see.

It looks spooky if some of the spaghetti pokes out of the eye holes!

Place the peppers on a baking sheet. Spoon some spaghetti into each pepper. Put the pepper tops back on and bake them in a medium oven for around half an hour.

You could make these spooky carrot fingers and dip, too. You need baby carrots, almonds, and some dip.

FINGER FOOD

Buy or make some dip. Hummus works well. Stick an almond to each carrot tip using a dab of the dip.

VEGGIE LION

YOU WILL NEED:
- a sliced butternut squash
- a sliced potato
- two small carrots
- one black olive
- fresh basil
- baking sheet
- cooking oil

Some people don't like eating vegetables. But who could resist this vegetable lion? It tastes really great. Try making your own animal designs from the same ingredients.

1

Ask an adult to help you cut these shapes from your butternut squash slices, carrots, and sliced potato.

2 Start creating your vegetable lion on a baking sheet. Make the head, body, and ears from squash. Make the cheeks and inner ears from potato slices. Add details using grated carrots, olive pieces, and basil stalks.

3 Arrange the carrot strips to make the legs and tail. Put fresh basil around the lion to make it look like he's in a jungle. You may prefer to add the basil after you cook the lion.

4 Brush a little cooking oil onto your lion. Place the baking sheet in a medium oven and cook for around fifteen minutes, until the squash and potato slices are soft. Arrange the basil and then serve.

COOL CUPCAKES

You can really have fun decorating cupcakes. Use any tiny candy or cake decorating goodies you might have in your cupboards. Here are some ideas.

Design Tips

To get the best result when creating the lace effect, use a small amount of sugar sifted very finely.

To create a lace pattern, find some lace or a doily. Place it on the cupcake. Sift a dusting of confectioner's sugar over the cake. Carefully remove the lace and you should see the pattern left on the cake.

MAKE FROSTING

Get 1 cup of butter and 4 cups of sugar. Mix the butter in a bowl to soften it a little. Gradually add in the sugar. You can add a spoon of milk, some food coloring, or a flavor if you want.

Decorate a cupcake with frosting and sprinkles. Cut out a shape in a piece of paper. Lay the paper gently on the frosting and pour the sprinkles. Place some larger sprinkles around the edge.

Buy or make some berry sauce. There is a recipe for berry sauce on page 9. Put the sauce in a squeezy bottle or pastry bag. Draw a spiral on your cupcake.

Place some large sprinkles or candy pieces along the spiral. If you have some tweezers, use them to help you position the sprinkles in just the right spot.

CHOCOLATE DELIGHT

You are going to need a spoon to enjoy this amazing chocolate treat! Have fun designing and decorating your dessert.

YOU WILL NEED:
- bar of chocolate
- 1 cup of milk
- chocolate syrup
- whipped cream
- a glass
- saucepan
- cheese grater

1

Finely grate most of a bar of chocolate into a bowl. Coarsely grate the rest of the bar and set it aside to use as a rim decoration later.

2

With an adult's help, pour the milk into a pan and add the finely grated chocolate. Gently heat the milk over a low heat. Stir regularly. Leave to cool.

3

While the chocolate mixture is cooling, drizzle a little chocolate syrup in a circle on a plate. Dip the rim of your glass into the syrup circle.

4

Put your grated chocolate onto another plate. Dip the syrup-covered glass rim into the chocolate. Carefully lift it out again and it should now have a ring of chocolate around the rim.

5

Once the chocolate in the pan is cool, pour it into the glass. Squirt some whipped cream in a swirl on top of the chocolate drink.

Design Tips

This chocolate delight is decorated with a vanilla stick and grated chocolate. You could use a tiny umbrella, or perhaps a cookie!

FRUITY SURPRISE

Fun drinks can add to the food design of your party. These two layered, liquid desserts look and taste fantastic!

YOU WILL NEED:
- orange juice
- pomegranate syrup such as grenadine
- ice cubes
- tall glass
- tiny umbrella
- cherry

Grenadine is a pomegranate-flavored syrup. It sinks to the bottom of the glass because it is heavier than the orange juice.

1

2

Put some ice in a tall glass, then fill it halfway with orange juice. Carefully pour some grenadine into the glass. The grenadine will sink to the bottom and create a sunset effect! Decorate with an umbrella and cherry.

YOU WILL NEED:
- a blue drink such as Gatorade or Kool-Aid
- pomegranate syrup such as grenadine
- milk
- vanilla ice cream
- a tall glass
- ice cubes

1

Chill the glass in the freezer for a few minutes. Add some ice cubes and the red pomegranate syrup.

2

In a jug, whisk a spoonful of vanilla ice cream into a small cup of milk. Pour gently into the glass.

3

Carefully pour in the blue drink to top off this dessert. You could add a piece of fresh pineapple for a fruity twist!

CREATURE CUPCAKES

Try making this monster cupcake. You can use the same basic design to make lots of different animal cupcakes.

YOU WILL NEED:
- a cupcake
- buttercream frosting
- a cookie
- large white chocolate candies
- some chocolate chips

1 If you are making your own frosting, the recipe is on page 23. Mix together all the ingredients for the frosting in a bowl.

2 To make the eyes, use a dab of frosting to stick two chocolate chips onto the white chocolate pieces.

Cover the cupcake with the frosting using a blunt knife. Regularly dipping the knife in water keeps it from sticking to the frosting.

Break the chocolate chip cookie in half. Now assemble your monster by pressing the eyes and cookie in place.

MAKE A PIG CUPCAKE

All you need is some pink frosting, some chocolate chips, and some pink marshmallows. Cover your cupcake in the frosting. Use one whole marshmallow for the snout. Use another two marshmallows for the ears. Then put the chocolate chips on for the nose and eyes.

Design Tips

To make the ears, squeeze the sides of the marshmallows together. Rip a tiny bit off one end. Then press the ripped end in the frosting.

GLOSSARY

antennae The movable organs of sensation on the head of an insect.

bacteria Microorganisms that live in soil, water, plants, and animals, and can cause disease.

chefs A head cook.

crockery Plates, dishes, cups, and similar items, usually made of clay or porcelain.

cutlery Utensils for cutting, serving, and eating food.

drizzle Trickle a thin stream of a liquid ingredient over food.

hygiene Conditions or practices, such as cleanliness, that are aids to good health.

pastry bag A hand-held bag made from cloth, paper, or plastic that is used to pipe semi-solid foods by pressing them through a narrow opening at one end.

presentation The way in which something is arranged or designed.

props Anything in a photograph near the subject that adds to the story and dimension of the picture.

sifted Passed through a sieve.

spatula An implement with a broad, flat, blunt blade, used for mixing and spreading things, especially in cooking and painting.

studio A room where an artist works.

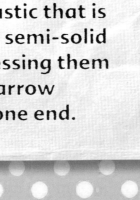

FOR MORE INFORMATION

Books

Cook, Deanna F. *Cooking Class: 57 Fun Recipes Kids Will Love to Make (and Eat!)* Storey Publishing, 2015.

Ryall, Jeanette. *Food Art (Awesome Art)*, Windmill Books, 2012.

Websites

Check out this fun site for healthy, yummy food design! **http://www.learnwithplayathome.com/p/food-for-kids.html**

Visit this delicious site for more fun, healthy foods! **http://www.superhealthykids.com/**

INDEX